EASY PIANO

JERRY LEE LEWIS

GREATEST HITS
Arranged by Bruce Nelson

M000098140

CONTENTS

JERRY LEE LEWIS:
A HALF-CENTURY OF HITS......................2

Breathless..14

Chantilly Lace 11

Great Balls of Fire 18

High School Confidential......................22

Me and Bobby McGee 28

Over the Rainbow...............................40

Rockin' My Life Away 35

What'd I Say 44

What's Made Milwaukee Famous
(Has Made a Loser Out of Me)............50

Whole Lotta Shakin' Going On 54

To my dearest Ann and Hannah

Alfred Music in association with Pont Neuf Music, Inc.,
Atway Music and Lost Square Music a division of
Brasstacks Alliance.

Photo: MICHAEL OCHS ARCHIVES.COM

JERRY LEE LEWIS: A HALF-CENTURY OF HITS

"Jerry Lee Lewis should be given an award for being himself."
—*Kris Kristofferson*

DECEMBER 4, 1956

He had given up his place at the piano stool, which probably didn't sit well with him, and he was staring over Carl Perkins's shoulder as Elvis Presley chorded the piano. Johnny Cash looked on. Then a photographer snapped Sun Records's Million Dollar Quartet. It was late in the afternoon of December 4, 1956.

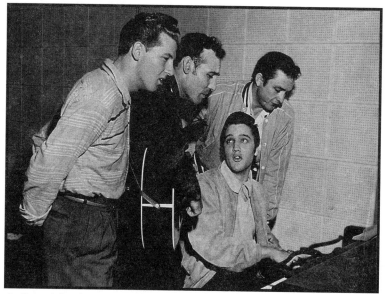

Left to right: Jerry Lee Lewis, Carl Perkins, Elvis Presley, Johnny Cash
(Photo: © Colin Escott)

Jimmie Rodgers, Al Jolson, Hank Williams, and himself. God-given talents, all of them. "Other people," Lewis once said, "they practice and they practice. These fingers of mine, they got brains in 'em. You don't tell them what to do; they do it."

In the 50 years since Lewis's first record was released, he has imprinted himself across the broad sweep of American music. His records never leave unanswered questions. From the first trill to the last imperious note, a Jerry Lee Lewis record can only be a Jerry Lee Lewis record. In all that time, he has barely written any songs. "All your great writers, it takes something out of you," he once said. "It's not worth it." But his interpretative skill is such that his records would be no more individualistic if he had written every word and scored every note.

Jerry Lee Lewis wasn't a star yet; his first record had been out just three days and he was there as Perkins's pianist. But far from being overawed in the presence of three stars, Lewis took the lead whenever he could and later asserted that Elvis had come to Sun especially to meet him. Elvis was coming off a career year and hadn't in fact returned to Sun to meet Lewis, but he was a fan by the time he left. "That boy can go," he told a reporter who had dropped by. "He has a different style and the way he plays piano just gets inside me." So Elvis was one of the first to know what we all now know.

There was a time when Lewis would have been voted the least likely survivor of the Million Dollar Quartet session, but now he's the last man standing. These days, his voice is careworn and his face betrays the heartbreak and tragedy that have always tempered the success, but his presence remains indomitable. For many years the myth of Jerry Lee Lewis has been inextricably confused with the story, and he seems to like it that way: the miles, the wives, the hits, the pills. It's the stuff of legend, and if anyone can truly say that he has done it *his* way, it's Jerry Lee Lewis. There are but four stylists in music, according to him, and he'll waste no time telling you who they are:

FERRIDAY

*Lewis: "I came into this world naked, feet first and jumpin'. I've been jumpin' ever since. I just am what I am. Jerry Lee F***ed Up Lewis. Anyone who doesn't like it can kiss my a**. I always done what I wanted to do and been what I wanted to be. I got music in my soul, rhythm in my veins, and a lotta thunder in my left hand. I can play music 'til it drives you insane. I'm the rockin'est muthahumper that's ever been."*

Lewis's mother, Mamie, stopped him from listening to records because she didn't want him sounding like anyone else. Every day, Jerry Lee would pound the old Starck upright piano, discovering something

2

that was inalienably his. The Lewises lived in Ferriday, Louisiana, and Jerry Lee was born on September 29, 1935, six months after his cousin Jimmy Swaggart, and six months before another cousin, Mickey Gilley. "I got the talent, you two got the scrapin's," Jerry Lee joked at a family reunion.

Lewis: "My family was poor. We grew up in a shack. We didn't even have a bathroom. My mother would pick cotton all day. It was real hard work for her, but she was a strong woman—physically and mentally. My daddy was a carpenter, a sharecropper, a bootlegger, and a construction worker. We moved home thirteen times one year. My daddy was a fantastic singer and guitar player. We would have family sessions all the time when I was a little boy. Gospel songs. My parents sang in church and I've never heard people that sang that good in my life."

Jerry Lee's father, Elmo, was in jail for bootlegging when Jerry Lee's older brother, Elmo Jr., was killed by a hit-and-run driver. Elmo Sr. was brought home in shackles for the funeral. From that point, it seemed as if all of Mamie's attention was focused on Jerry Lee. Perhaps he would amount to something and deliver them all.

Jerry Lee's early years revolved around Saturday morning shoot-'em-ups, Sunday morning church, surreptitious trips to the local black juke joints, and the piano. Always the piano. Mamie went deep into debt to buy the Starck upright. Jerry Lee played it until he literally wore the ivory off the keys. He loved the gentle lilt of old pop songs, the fury of traveling evangelists, the inexpressible sadness of country music, and the boisterousness of roadhouse R&B. It came out as rock 'n' roll.

In June 1949, Lewis made his first public appearance at the opening of Babin-Paul Motors in Ferriday. He performed a country hit of the day, Bill Nettles's "Hadacol Boogie," and an R&B hit, "Drinkin' Wine Spo-Dee-O-Dee." Both stayed in his memory after that, and both are reprised here. Hadacol, incidentally, was a foul-tasting patent medicine that contained alcohol and laxative in equally large doses; it was the closest thing to a nip you could get in "dry" areas of the South.

In the spring of 1952, Lewis and his best friend, Cecil Harrelson, went to New Orleans because they had never been. At the corner of Rampart and Dumaine Streets they found the J&M Studio. It was where the

area's R&B stars, notably Fats Domino, recorded, but, like most studios, it had a sideline in "record your own voice" discs. Home recording was in its infancy, so the only way most singers could hear how they sounded was to make a private recording in a professional studio. (That's why Elvis first went to Sun.) Lewis saw J&M and decided to hear how he sounded. Harrelson paid two dollars, and Lewis cut Lefty Frizzell's then current hit "Don't Stay Away ('Til Love Grows Cold)" and an improvised boogie. Recorded four and a half years before Lewis's first commercial session, it's a very assured debut.

At one time or another, Cecil Harrelson has been Lewis's best friend, brother-in-law, and manager. For many years, whenever he left his house, he would bring along the 1952 disc in a battered briefcase. The disc was a "one-off" recording in that it was recorded directly to an acetate disc. There were no safety copies and no file copies in the studio. Often, acetates can be played only a few times before the coating flakes off the aluminium disc, but somehow this acetate survived 54 years. Transferring acetates is an art in itself. Only a handful of studios in the United States can make a successful transfer, and one of them is the Country Music Hall of Fame's media center. The Hall of Fame's engineer, Alan Stoker, is the son of Jordanaire Gordon Stoker (for many years, the Jordanaires backed Elvis, Patsy Cline, and many others in Nashville studios). On January 31, 2006, Harrelson drove to Nashville with Lewis' attorney, Beth Cocke, and Harrelson handed over the acetate. Stoker cleaned it, tested it to determine the best stylus for the groove width, and transferred it to digital media for Time Life. Inevitably, there was some surface noise, but the sound was vibrant and clear, transporting Harrelson back to the J&M Studio in New Orleans in the spring of 1952.

Shortly before the New Orleans trip, Lewis married for the first time. Dorothy Barton was a preacher's daughter. She and Lewis dropped out of school together, and Lewis followed his new father-in-law into the ministry. He enrolled at the Southwestern Bible Institute (now the Southwestern Assemblies of God

University) in Waxahachie, Texas. Lewis has always said that he was expelled for jazzing up the hymn "My God Is Real."

Lewis: "I kinda put a little feelin' into it. A little Louisiana boogie-woogie. The students all clapped and rose to their feet, but the dean expelled me. I come home. Momma said, 'You're a preacher now.' I read the Bible, wrote sermons. I thought, 'Waxahachie can kiss my a**.'"

Across the river in Natchez, Mississippi, Lewis worked the clubs, and it was there that he met his second wife, Jane Mitcham.

Lewis: "We was havin' fun, then she became pregnant. Boy oh boy. I was still married to Dorothy. Jane's brothers arrived in town with horsewhips and guns, so I done the decent thing and I married her. That was one week before my divorce from Dorothy."

In 1954, the Lewises had a son, Jerry Lee Jr. Trying to support his young family, Lewis sold vacuum cleaners door-to-door, but music was never far from his thoughts, and Elvis's first Sun record turned his head around. "Wow," he told Jane, "looka right here, I don't know who this dude is, but someone just done opened the door." Later that year Lewis drove to Shreveport, where Elvis was making a name for himself on *The Louisiana Hayride*. The show's emcee allowed Lewis to make another demonstration record as an audition for a Slim Whitman tour, but didn't encourage him to stay. A little later, Lewis went to Nashville. Pianists were rare in Nashville circa 1955, and his reception was as frosty as it had been in Shreveport. Only Webb Pierce's supporting act, pianist Roy Hall, offered a glimmer of hope when he allowed Lewis to fill in for him at an after-hours nightspot. Hall had just recorded an R&B tune, "Whole Lot of Shakin' Going On," and Lewis returned to Ferriday and Natchez with what he could remember of that song echoing in his mind.

By 1956, Elvis was no longer on Sun Records or *The Louisiana Hayride*; he was the biggest star in popular music. In *Country Song Roundup*, Lewis read how Sam Phillips at Sun in Memphis had discovered Elvis. Surely if Phillips had the intuition to respond to Elvis, he would understand Jerry Lee Lewis. Memphis was an easy drive, so Elmo Lewis sold eggs and Jerry Lee saved a little money from his club dates to pay for the trip and they drove on up.

SUN

Sam Phillips was out of town the day that Jerry Lee Lewis arrived at Sun, and Jack Clement was in the control room. "The receptionist brought Jerry Lee back to me," Clement said later. "She said, 'I've got a fella here who says he plays piano like Chet Atkins.' I thought I'd better listen to that. I believe he was playing piano with his right hand and drums with his left. I made a tape because he was different. I took his name and told him I'd let Sam hear the tape when he got back, but after Jerry left, I started listening to the tape and it really grew on me." Clement was a skilled musician, and saw that Lewis's bravado enabled him to get away with things that others couldn't. "He was unique as a piano player," said Clement. "He doesn't care if he hits a bad note. It doesn't bother him a bit. He thinks that everything he plays is great and because of that, it is."

On November 14, 1956, Clement called in Lewis and some other musicians for a formal session, then held onto the tape until Phillips's return. "I don't know if I'd told Jack this," Phillips said later, "but I had been wanting to get off this guitar scene and show that it could be done with other instruments. They put that tape on and I said, 'Where in hell did this man come from?' He played that piano with abandon. A lot of people do that, but I could hear, between the stuff that he played and didn't play, that spiritual thing. I told Jack, 'Just get him in here as fast as you can.'" Clement didn't even have to call; Lewis returned with a song that he had written, "End of the Road," and Phillips immediately scheduled the first Jerry Lee Lewis record. It was released on December 1, 1956.

Elmo returned to Ferriday, while Jerry Lee hustled a few gigs around Memphis and slept on J. W. Brown's couch. Brown was Mamie's sister's son, and he had moved to Memphis in 1950. By then, he had a daughter, Myra Gail, who was twelve when Lewis moved in with them. Lewis felt sure he was falling in love with her and she with him.

At every opportunity, Lewis went to play for Phillips. They were destined to come together, the former divinity student and the former mortician's assistant. Phillips understood that he must let Lewis play song after song to find the one that held promise. That's how "Whole Lot of Shakin' Going On" came to be recorded. In the opening four bars, Lewis made the piano into a percussion instrument. Phillips's contribution was to feed the signal back on itself at just the right increment of tape delay, fattening the sound to the point where the record throbbed with its own hypnotic life by the time the drums came in. It became Lewis's second record and first hit, but was pegging out halfway up the charts when Lewis made his first network television appearance on *The Steve Allen Show*. That night, Sunday, July 28, 1957, was a landmark in rock 'n' roll history: the intensity went up a notch. Lewis hammered the piano, eyes fixed above. Then he glared at the camera with wild-eyed fury: "Whose barn? MAH barn!" "Shakin'" resumed its upward movement, eventually peaking at No. 3.

The record's impact was felt far beyond the United States. "I was walking through Pontypridd, where I come from in South Wales," remembered Tom Jones, "and I was with some of my friends and we were talking about rock 'n' roll and all of a sudden "Whole Lot of Shakin'" comes out of the loudspeaker outside of the record shop and my friend said, 'Is that what you're talking about?' and I said, 'That's *exactly* what I'm talking about!'"

Lewis: "When Mister Phillips gimme my first royalty check for "Whole Lot of Shakin'," he put on an extra thousand dollars. I could see a nice Cadillac in a car window someplace and go in and buy me one. There was money comin' in from every direction. I never had no money before, and I didn't know what to do with it. I went home and bought my kinfolk anything they wanted. My cousin, Jimmy Swaggart, come over and asked if I'd get him a car. I took him to the Ford place, but Jimmy said he didn't want no Ford. He wanted an Oldsmobile."

Up in New York, songwriter Otis Blackwell, who had written Elvis's "Don't Be Cruel" and "All Shook Up," was asked to write some songs and find some artists for a low-budget rock movie, *Jamboree*. "I went to a friend's record store in Brooklyn and listened to records in his back room," Blackwell told Ralph Newman. "I must have listened to one hundred records until I came across this record. He only had one copy of it, way in the back. I took it to the producer and said, 'I'm gonna tell you, man, I hear this dude as being one of the top artists. Maybe even bigger than Presley!' It was "Whole Lot of Shakin' Going On." They approached him and got him, and a few days later, a writer named Jack Hammer brought me a group song

called "Great Balls of Fire." I liked the title, so I said, 'Give me the title, I'll write the song.'"

It's a testament to Lewis's genius that he could take a slight song manufactured for an equally slight movie and transform it into one of the era's classics. Some claim to hear a rhythm guitar, but it's essentially Jerry Lee Lewis and drums. If there's a third "instrument," it's Phillips's reverberation, adding depth and presence. "You can recut 'Great Balls of Fire,'" Phillips said later. "Big digital sounds and all that s***, but that just won't get it. Just go back to the original and listen to the spontaneity. How are you going to improve upon perfection?" The B side was Hank Williams's "You Win Again," and 10 years later, it would enable Lewis to tell interviewers that he had always been country.

Blackwell wrote Lewis's follow-up, "Breathless." In a tie-in between Sun, Dick Clark, and Beech-Nut chewing gum, kids could send in 50 cents and five Beech-Nut wrappers to receive a "free, autographed" copy of "Breathless." Even minor Sun artists were put to work autographing and shipping the record. When Lewis sang, "I burn like a wood in flame," it came out as, "I *boin* like a wood in flame." Ten years later John Fogerty sang, "Proud Mary keep on *boinin'*." They didn't talk like that in Northern California, where Fogerty was from, but they did in Louisiana. The B side, "Down the Line," was written by a hard-luck Sun artist named Roy Orbison.

Lewis's last top-20 pop hit titled another quickie exploitation movie, *High School Confidential*, starring Mamie Van Doren. The film was supposed to be an exposé of the high school drug problem (*yes*, there was a high school drug problem in 1958). Try as he might, songwriter Ron Hargrave couldn't work the title into the song, and surrendered half of his writer's share to Lewis. It was released just as Lewis left for a tour of England in May of 1958.

The European tour should have broadened Lewis's success, but six months earlier, he had snuck off to Hernando, Mississippi, to marry Myra Gail Brown. The Lewises arrived in London, and the press picked up a chance remark from one of the entourage about Lewis's wife being rather young. Within days, Lewis was greeted with jeers at his concerts. Talking to journalists at London's Westbury Hotel, Lewis only made things worse. "I was a bigamist at the age of 16," he told the *Daily Express*. "I have not told the full truth before, but last night I had an abusive phone call from my second wife, Jane Mitcham. I decided that if she wants to play it that way, so will I." There were questions in the British House of Commons. "Is the minister aware of the great offense caused to many people by the arrival of this man with his 13-year-old bride? Are you not aware that we have more than enough rock 'n' roll entertainers of our own without importing them from overseas?" And that's why stars have media handlers today.

Many of Lewis's friends and family married young. He couldn't understand the fuss, and believed that he would return home to find that the disclosures would have no impact. He couldn't have been more wrong. "I think that somebody out there was looking for a place to stick the knife in rock 'n' roll and Jerry provided 'em a real good place," Myra said later. "They pulled Jerry's records off the air. They cancelled TV shows. They cancelled dates. He was making thousands and thousands of dollars a night and he went back to working for two or three hundred dollars." Sam Phillips was equally devastated. "He was the hottest thing going. I think Jerry's innocence back then, trying to be open and friendly and engaging with press, backfired. They scalped him. So many people wanted to do in rock 'n' roll, and this was just what they were looking for. It should never have played a role of such significance in Jerry's life."

"God," Lewis said later, "I didn't know the hole could be that deep." Three years passed before he placed another record in the top 30, and it was a version of Ray Charles's recent hit "What'd I Say." The follow-ups sputtered and died, just as Sun itself was slowly dying.

Lewis: "When the DJs stopped playing my records, I never said anything. What could I do? Holler and scream at 'em? For a while they wasn't playing Elvis, Chuck Berry, or none of them. You'd think rock 'n' roll had died in the night. All they played was them Bobbys—Bobby Vee, Bobby Vinton, Bobby Rydell, Bobby Darin. If your name was Bobby, you were in with a sporting chance. I must be the only artist in the world who's been down as many times as I have. I mean down to rock bottom. I was making ten thousand a night, and got knocked back to two-fifty. I couldn't care less. Money don't mean nothin' to me."

Things only got worse. Over Easter 1962, Jerry Lee and Myra's son, Steve Allen Lewis, died in a tragic pool accident. Jerry Lee was in the middle of a return trip to England, and Myra, heartbroken, flew to join him. She was just 17, and must have felt as if she had lived a lifetime. Stevie's death caused problems in their marriage, but their daughter, Phoebe Allen Lewis, was born 16 months later. In fact, she was born the week that Jerry Lee left Sun Records. Lewis and Sam Phillips had argued about royalties, they'd argued about promotion, they'd argued about religion, and they'd argued about arguing. The Sun contract was up in 1963, and Lewis wanted to move on. His last single on the Sun label was a rocked-up minstrel song from 1878, "Carry Me Back to Ol' Virginia." Three other songs were recorded at that session: "One Minute Past Eternity," "Invitation to Your Party," and "I Can't Seem to Say Goodbye." They weren't released at the time, but within five years, Lewis would be in the country charts with a very similar sound. It's almost as if the answer to his problems was right there, but no one saw it.

When fans asked Lewis if anything remained unreleased from his tenure at Sun, he would reply that he had left enough for forty albums…and he wasn't too far off the mark. Excavations of the Sun vaults have yielded treasures like Johnny O'Keefe's Australian hit "Real Wild Child (Wild One)," the lascivious blues "Big Leg Woman," and Roy Acuff's "Night Train to Memphis." Who but Jerry Lee Lewis could make such diverse songs into a unified musical statement?

SMASH

In September 1963, Jerry Lee Lewis signed with the Smash division of Mercury Records. Producer Shelby Singleton put out the call for new material, and the New York team that had written one of Mercury's biggest hits of 1963, the Angels's "My Boyfriend's Back," came up with "I'm on Fire." Mercury held the presses, thinking they had found Lewis's comeback hit, and it might have happened if the Beatles hadn't just arrived in America, changing radio playlists almost overnight. Mercury didn't really know what to do with Lewis after that. R&B, soul, rock—nothing clicked. He made an early return to country music with the *Country Songs for City Folks* LP. One of the few sales was to Lewis's longtime fan, Tom Jones, who immediately copied the arrangement of "Green, Green Grass of Home" and transformed it into a top-20 hit.

In an odd reversal of fate, Lewis became a conquering hero in Europe. His return there coincided with his son's death, but if anything lifted his spirits, it was the tumultuous reception he received overseas. He returned almost every year thereafter and became a hero to those who put grease in their hair. His shows redefined the performing art of rock 'n' roll.

European concert receipts didn't impress Mercury Records, and in 1968 the company decided to drop Lewis when his five-year contract expired that September. Singleton, who had been Lewis's champion at Mercury, had departed to start his own label and was on the point of buying Sun Records. That left Lewis in the hands of fellow Louisianan, Jerry Kennedy, who took up a suggestion from a DJ in Knoxville that Lewis cut an all-country session with new songs. Lewis had tried to do just that at his last Sun session, but the songs were still unreleased, and the Country Songs for City Folks album was all standards. Kennedy's promo man, Eddie Kilroy, found "Another Place, Another Time." As it climbed the charts, promoters looked for Lewis and discovered him in Los Angeles playing Iago in a rock 'n' roll version of Othello. Fortunately, the show did poorly and closed, otherwise Lewis wouldn't have been able to support the record and it might not have done as well as it did.

"Sales were so strong, Mercury thought it was a pop hit," said Kennedy. "We needed a follow-up, and I put out the call to music publishers. Al Gallico was a publisher and he had a writer named Glenn Sutton. He'd call Glenn and say, 'Have you got a song for Jerry Lee Lewis?' Glenn would say, 'Yeah, I'm working on it.' One Sunday morning Gallico phoned Glenn, and Glenn was hungover, and he said, 'I got it, Al.' He didn't have a thing, but he was looking at a beer ad in the paper. He said, 'The Beer That Made Milwaukee Famous Has Made a Loser out of Me.' He changed it to "What's Made Milwaukee Famous (Has Made a Loser out of Me)." Big record. It even got in the bottom of the pop charts, and Jerry Lee saw it, and he called Billboard magazine and told them to take it out of the pop charts. Called the pop editor and said, 'You wouldn't back me when I was down. Take my record out of those damn pop charts.' I couldn't believe it."

Lewis: "It was a way to get in through the back door, to get the disc jockeys to play my records again. I went country, but to me, I was still a rock 'n' roller. But I lived a lot of those songs. As the years go by, you get into it. You've lived it."

Suddenly the hits came in abundance. Top country songwriters were holding their best songs for the next Jerry Lee Lewis session. Mercury picked up their option on his services, and Singleton, now the owner of Sun Records, began issuing the songs from the last Sun session. More hits. Lewis began telling the press that he had always been country. Not entirely true, but who would begrudge him this success after 10 years in the wilderness?

"What's Made Milwaukee Famous" reached No. 2; "To Make Love Sweeter for You" reached No. 1; and one of Lewis's Memphis pals, Bill Taylor, wrote a song about a man trapped in a hopeless affair with a married woman, "There Must Be More to Love Than This," and it too topped the country charts. Kennedy didn't dare release an up-tempo single because he couldn't risk radio programmers declaring that Lewis was returning to his rockabilly past. Up-tempo songs, like Merle Haggard's blue-collar anthem, "Workin' Man Blues," were consigned to LPs.

Kennedy liked to record in closed sessions, and winced when Lewis arrived with a retinue of hangers-on. "It was all we could do to stop them burping or opening beer cans on tape," said Kennedy's partner, Charlie Fach. Eventually, Kennedy came to appreciate that Lewis needed an audience. "Bad as I hated it, he did better with a crowd," he admitted later. "I can remember 70 or 80 people in the control room and standing around in the studio. One time, we almost had a song nailed and there was a thunk right at the end. Some guy had left the studio and slammed the door. The engineer went down and was chewing him out. 'Why'd you do that?' The guy said, 'The ice in Jerry's drink was melting.'"

As always, personal tragedy and public scandal combined to cast a pall over the success. Lewis's beloved mother, Mamie, died in 1971, just as Myra Gail began divorce proceedings. Together, those events sent Lewis reeling, and he decided to follow in the footsteps of his cousin Jimmy Swaggart and once again become a man of God. Mercury hastily concocted a desperate Plan B to market him as a gospel artist, but for reasons unrevealed, Lewis soon returned to the only life he had ever really known.

Since the country breakthrough in 1968, Lewis's records had been spare, unornamented and unremittingly slow-paced. After three years, Kennedy decided to break out of the artistic straitjacket. When

Lewis arrived at Mercury's studio in August 1971, he was greeted by a 10-piece string section rehearsing a Kris Kristofferson song. Kennedy wanted to give the big-budget treatment to "Me and Bobby McGee." The song had been a country hit for Roger Miller and a pop hit for Janis Joplin, and so if Lewis was to do it, he would have to rethink it. And that's what he did. In losing Kristofferson's whimsicality, he created a new song.

Lewis's big-budget, amped-up "Me and Bobby McGee" became a pop and country hit at an opportune moment. Vintage rock 'n' roll was experiencing a rebirth. It had been less than 15 years since Buddy Holly's death was heralded as the symbolic finale of the rock 'n' roll era. The music had changed beyond all recognition since then, and the revival was for those who couldn't stomach the new stuff. For many '50s artists, the revival was a lifeline, but Lewis didn't need to trade endlessly on the hits he had enjoyed in 1957 and '58; he did, however, need to rock. At a session in February 1972, he tackled an old favorite. "Out of nowhere," remembered Jerry Kennedy's assistant, Roy Dea, "Jerry said, 'Let's do "Chantilly Lace."' The arranger said, 'We don't have charts.' Jerry said, 'We're just running it down. Don't worry 'bout the mules. Just load the wagon.' The arranger just about had a heart attack. Jerry Lee took off his turtleneck sweater. Played it twice."

Lewis: "Sam Phillips's brother, Jud, was managing me. He was well-oiled on that session. Just before he passed out on the floor he said, 'You gotta do "Chantilly Lace."' I told him I didn't even know "Chantilly Lace." He said, 'Well, make it up.' I did one take on it."

"Chantilly Lace" was a lewd song, but its originator, the Big Bopper (who had perished alongside Buddy Holly), had played it for laughs. When Lewis said, "Oh, baby, that's what I like," it was abundantly clear what "that" was. If Kennedy had misgivings, he needn't have. Released as a single, the song topped the country charts and reached No. 43 on the pop charts.

Mercury began to think that Lewis's country success could be a springboard back to the pop charts. He was brought to London in January 1973 to work with super-star guests like Peter Frampton and Rory Gallagher.

Lewis: "I walked in. I seen all these cats standing around. Real long hair and everythin'. I turned to Junior

[Jerry Lee Lewis Jr.—his son by Jane Mitcham—who came along as a drummer] and I said, 'Boy, have I made a mistake comin' over here.' I sat down at the piano, put the headphones on and started to record. These kids, there wasn't any one of them smokin' pot, takin' any pills or liquor. They were clean. Real nice, and they were the greatest musicians I ever heard."

The master and his disciples (the age difference was not that great—just a few years, in most cases) brought a fresh slant to rock and blues standards, including the song that had set Lewis on his path, "Drinkin' Wine Spo-Dee-O-Dee." It reached No. 41 on the pop charts almost 25 years after Lewis had first performed it at Babin-Paul Motors and his dad had passed the hat. The follow-up, "No Headstone on My Grave," was a song that Charlie Rich had written when both he and Lewis were scuffling at Sun.

Shortly after returning from London, Lewis made his debut on the Grand Ole Opry. It was 18 years since he had left Nashville broke and disheartened; if only all of life's disappointments could be reversed so deftly. But for all the success (65 country hits at last counting), Lewis was never truly accepted in Nashville. He didn't move there and didn't schmooze there. He didn't fit in with the family values crowd. Lewis family values weren't necessarily worse, but they were different. Three top-10 pop hits made Lewis one of the charter inductees into the Rock and Roll Hall of Fame, but he has yet to be inducted into the Country Music Hall of Fame.

Mercury's plan to broaden Lewis's success didn't work. The hits tailed off, just as Lewis's personal life seemed on the verge of once again spiraling out of control. In 1973, he was jailed and fined for driving while intoxicated. Just after his release, his son Junior was killed when a car he was towing jack-knifed and hit the abutment of a bridge near Hernando, Mississippi. Three weeks later, Lewis's fourth wife, Jaren, filed for divorce.

A change came over many of Lewis's later Mercury recordings. He found songwriters who understood his feelings, and he in turn etched himself indelibly on their words. Mack Vickery's "That Kind of Fool" elicited one of Lewis's most heartfelt performances. The regret was almost palpable. In June 1975, Lewis arrived at Mercury's Nashville studio with his voice almost shot. Kris Kristofferson's keyboard player, Donnie Fritts, had written a song especially for him, "A Damn Good Country Song." Lewis turned in an artlessly affecting performance. As always, the remorse was tempered with arrogance.

"Middle Age Crazy" was the last big country hit on Mercury, and it came in 1978. Sonny Throckmorton had written a short story song about a self-made man getting over his midlife crisis with a fling. "I didn't know anything about being middle age crazy at the time," Throckmorton admitted later. "I wasn't old enough. Then when I passed 40, I went through the whole deal." Lewis told an interviewer that he had been middle age crazy at 15, a statement that, like many of his off-the-cuff remarks, was truer than it seemed. The session coincided with one of Lewis's first hospitalizations. "Oh, man, he was white as a sheet," said Jerry Kennedy. "I was surprised we got anything from him." Released immediately after the session, "Middle Age Crazy" leaped to No. 4 on the country charts and gave Lewis his best showing since "Chantilly Lace." The song later became one of those rare instances of a song inspiring a movie (starring Ann-Margret and Bruce Dern) rather than vice versa.

On "Middle Age Crazy," Lewis overdubbed his vocal to a pre-recorded track. He wasn't even playing piano. It wasn't the way he liked to work.

Lewis: "'Middle Age Crazy' was one of the last things Mercury done on me. That's why I left the company. You're losing out on something when you record like that. But it was a great record."

It was a very different Jerry Lee Lewis who left Mercury in 1978, 15 years after he had signed with the label. The endless party and endless highway had taken their toll. "I've lost my mother," he told interviewer Jim Neff around that time. "Lost my two sons. Nobody knows that feeling until they walk by the casket and see flesh and blood lying there. It's a hard pill to swallow. You can't get over it. I thought I was indestructible. I thought the world had finally come up with a superman. I come to find out I wasn't."

ROCKIN' MY LIFE AWAY

Jerry Kennedy made no attempt to keep Lewis under contract. "I thought it was healthy that he left," he said. "He was tired." Elektra Records's Nashville division wanted him. Instead of recording in Nashville,

Lewis was sent to California to work with Bones Howe, who had produced Elvis's 1968 comeback TV special. Howe assembled some top players, including Elvis's guitarist, James Burton. "We're going to have to do the album in four days," Howe told Lewis. "What are we gonna do the other two days?" Lewis replied.

The first Elektra album, simply and enigmatically titled *Jerry Lee Lewis*, was an astonishing return to form. Once again Lewis was recording "live" in the studio. Critic Robert Christgau called it "autumnal rock 'n' roll," but we should all wish the September of our years to be so wild and productive. The song selection was inspired, including Bob Dylan's "Rita May." "Who wrote that?" asked Lewis. "Bob Dylan," said Howe. Lewis appeared not to know who Dylan was. "That boy's good," he said. "I'll do anything by him." Lewis had been known to taunt record label people, and might have been having a private joke at Howe's expense, but then again, he might not.

Mack Vickery had written "Rockin' My Life Away" for and about Jerry Lee Lewis. The message was clear: Elvis might be gone, but "my name is Jerry Lee Lewis and I'm durn sure here to stay." It was part affirmation, part threat. The song began obscurely with "14, 25, 40, 98," leaving listeners wondering if Lewis was garbling words or dates, but Vickery later told interviewers that he wanted the song to begin with a quarterback calling signals as if Lewis were shouting out the game plan for his life in a code only he could understand.

The other songs on the album included Charlie Rich's gin-sodden "Who Will the Next Fool Be." Like "No Headstone," it was a song that Rich had written when he and Lewis were languishing at Sun, wondering if they would ever get another hit. Lewis turned the song into a poisoned dart hurled at every woman who had done him wrong. Critics loved the album, but sales were disappointing.

Lewis: "When I cut that first Elektra album, Daddy was passing away. We got through the last song, and I was told my Daddy died, and I went on home. Elektra had given me a $300,000 guarantee an album, and they got mad about that."

Trying to salvage the deal, Elektra brought Lewis to Nashville and placed him with Eddie Kilroy, who had been Jerry Kennedy's promo man (he currently programs country music for Sirius satellite radio).

Kilroy took aim at the country charts with "Thirty-Nine and Holding" and "I'd Do It All Again," but was sufficiently moved by Lewis's performance of Judy Garland's, "Over the Rainbow" to schedule it as a single. In most versions, "Over the Rainbow" is a profoundly optimistic song, looking forward rather than back, but in Lewis's hands, it's a lament for what should have been rather than a vision of what might be: "There was a rainbow ol' Jerry dreamed of once upon a lullaby."

And then Elektra Records's Nashville division was taken over by Jimmy Bowen. Instead of appreciating the chance to work with someone from his era, Bowen saw no chance of recouping the $300,000 Lewis was to be paid for his next four albums. In his autobiography, Bowen says he offered Lewis $350,000 to leave the label, then tells an astonishing tale of sending some of his guys to mollify Lewis, only to have him pull a gun on them. "Then he muttered something about killing me," Bowen writes. If anything, the story became even more bizarre as Bowen sent a crew to tap Lewis's phone to gather evidence, only to find the FBI already tapping it for other reasons.

If half the stories are half true, these were Lewis's troubled years. His life was a gift to the tabloids. Elvis's former "personal physician," George Nichopoulos, was in Lewis's retinue before being indicted by the Tennessee Board of Medical Examiners for overprescribing. There were lawsuits, hospitalizations, marriages, divorces, the unexplained death of Lewis's fifth wife, the accidental shooting of his bass player, and IRS troubles that landed him in exile in Ireland for a while. Lewis could still laugh at it all, though. Playing a gig at the Palomino in Los Angeles, he stared into the audience and said, "Elvis killed himself over a broad. It took five of 'em to put me in the shape I'm in today." In April 1984, he married his sixth wife, Kerrie McCarver, with whom he had a son, Jerry Lee Lewis III. In 1994, Lewis returned to the U.S. from Ireland and negotiated a settlement with the IRS. Ironically, after the acrimony associated with his departure from Elektra's Nashville division, he signed a deal with Elektra's Sire Records that yielded one album, *Young Blood*. In the photographs and in the self-penned liner notes, Lewis seemed very much a man at peace. The title gave every reviewer a cheap shot, but Andy Paley's production was spare and to the point, and the reception was good. Songs from Lewis's childhood like "Down the Road a Piece" and Jimmie Rodgers's "Miss the Mississippi and You" sat comfortably alongside newer songs like "It Was the Whiskey Talkin' (Not Me)" (a song that he had recorded for the *Dick Tracy* soundtrack) and "Crown Victoria Custom '51."

In June 2005, Lewis and Kerrie McCarver Lewis divorced. "It's been a long day, and an expensive day," Lewis joked as he left the courtroom, but the divorce freed him up to accept bookings, so there's a good chance he will once again come to a theater near you. In his 70th year, he can still turn in a master class in rock 'n' roll.

Lewis: "I like good whiskey, good workin' women, and good music. If God made anything better than a woman, he kept it for himself. He gave man a woman to love, and I've done the best I can. When the Lord's book is opened, we'll stand before Him and be judged. He will judge me. No man or woman can. I don't question God, but He don't scare me worth a damn. If it's Hell I'm going to, I'll face it, but I don't think I've done no wrong."

Had Jerry Lee Lewis been born 100 years earlier, he would have been a minstrel in a traveling show; instead he's a rock 'n' roller who could never quite get the country out of his soul, and a country singer who could never forget that he was once rock 'n' roll's best and brightest star. Like the minstrels of old, he is a natural born entertainer. He has dominated every stage he has walked upon for 50 years, and outlasted those who have prophesied his own doom along with that of his music.

—Colin Escott
Nashville, January 2006

Colin Escott is the author of *Good Rockin' Tonight: The Story of Sun Records*, *Hank Williams: The Biography*, and an anthology of music journalism, *Tattooed on Their Tongues*. He co-wrote and co-produced the PBS/BBC documentary *Hank Williams: Honky Tonk Blues*.

Reprinted by permission of Time/Life from the Jerry Lee Lewis box set *A Half-Century of Hits*

CHANTILLY LACE

Words and Music by J.P. Richardson
Arranged by Bruce Nelson

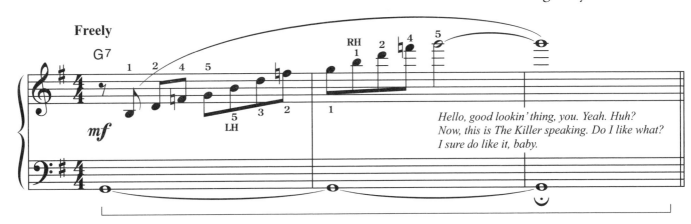

*Hello, good lookin' thing, you. Yeah. Huh?
Now, this is The Killer speaking. Do I like what?
I sure do like it, baby.*

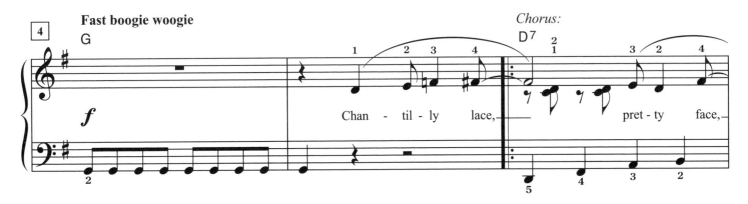

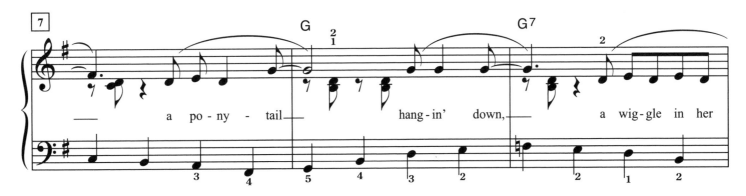

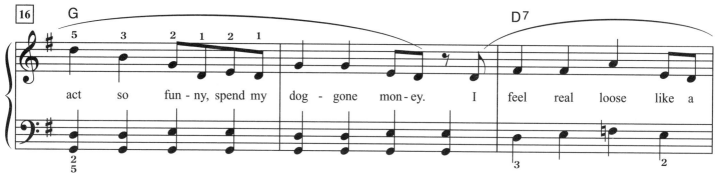

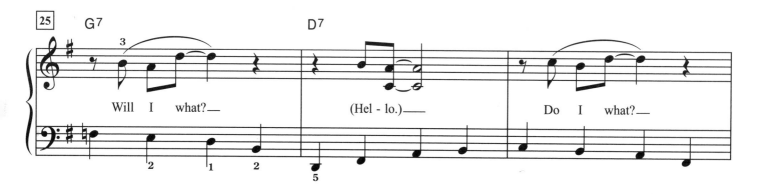

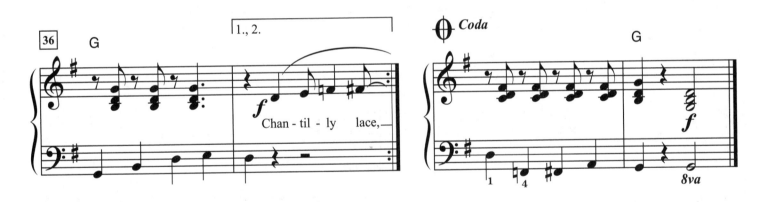

Bridge 2:
(Spoken:) Huh? Ha ha ha. Huh? What say?
Pick you up at eight? And don't be late?
You gotta be jokin', woman.
I thought you might pick me up at eight-and-don't-be-late.
It don't make no diff'rence, baby; you know what Jerry Lee likes.
(To Chorus:)

Bridge 3:
(Spoken:) Whoo, ha ha ha ha ha ha.
Honey, you tearin' me up on this telephone.
I swear I don't know what in the world I'm gonna do with you.
You, you yap and yap and yap and yap and yap,
But when you break it all down, you know what I like.

14

BREATHLESS

Words and Music by Otis Blackwell
Arranged by Bruce Nelson

GREAT BALLS OF FIRE

Words and Music by
Otis Blackwell and Jack Hammer
Arranged by Bruce Nelson

HIGH SCHOOL CONFIDENTIAL

Words and Music by
Jerry Lee Lewis and Ron Hargrave
Arranged by Bruce Nelson

23

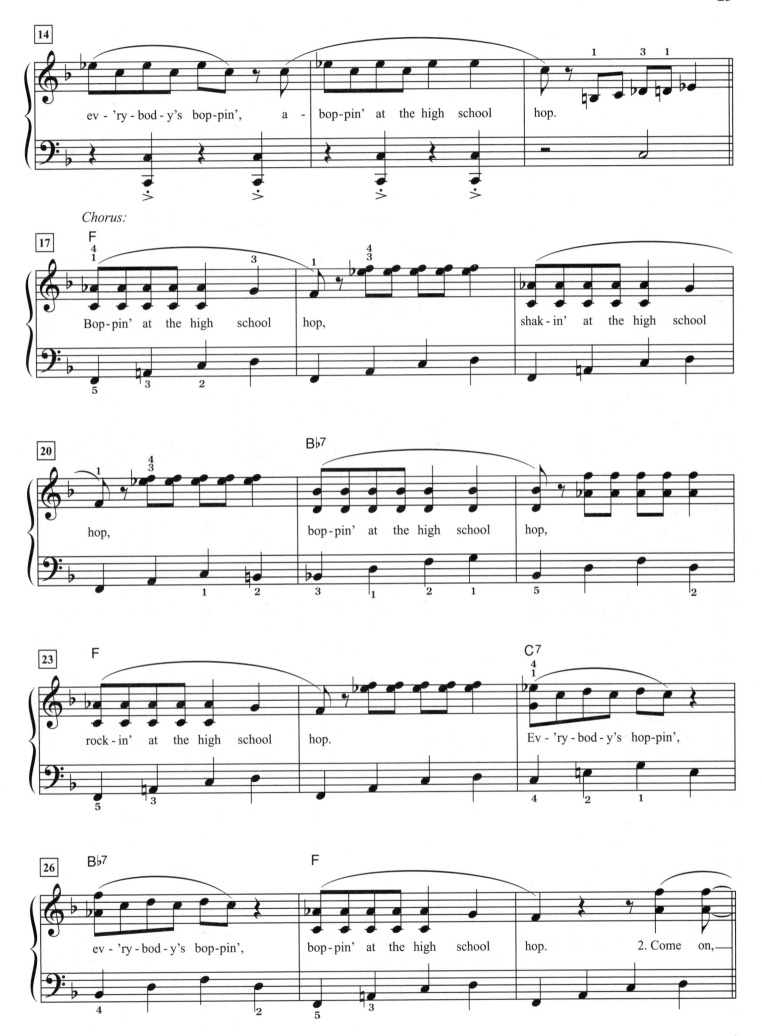

hop,

shak - in' at the high school hop,

mov - in' at the high school hop.

Ev - 'ry - bod - y's bop - pin',

ev - 'ry - bod - y's rock - in',

bop - pin' at the high school bop.

Solo:

ME AND BOBBY MCGEE

Words and Music by
Kris Kristofferson and Fred Foster
Arranged by Bruce Nelson

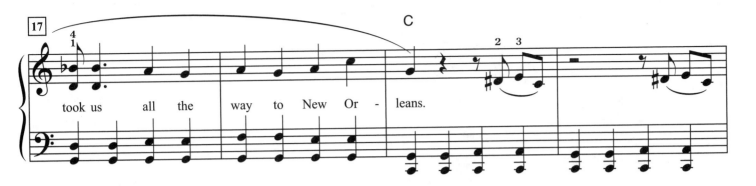

took us all the way to New Or - leans.

Pulled my old har - poon out of my dirt - y red ban - dan - na, —

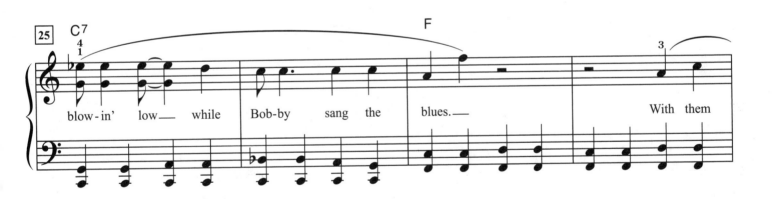

blow - in' low — while Bob - by sang the blues. — With them

wind - shield wip - ers slap pin' time — and Bob - by clap - pin' hands with mine, —

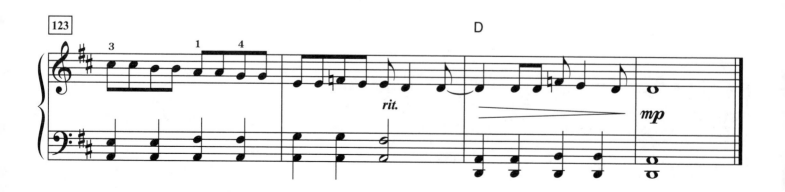

ROCKIN' MY LIFE AWAY

Words and Music by Mack Vickery
Arranged by Bruce Nelson

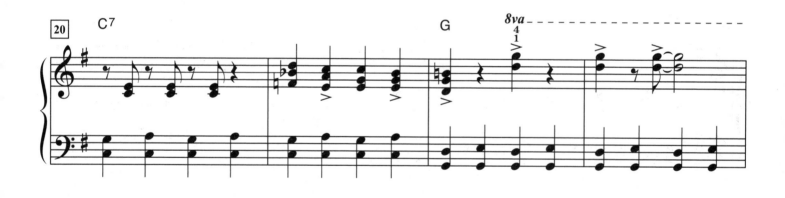

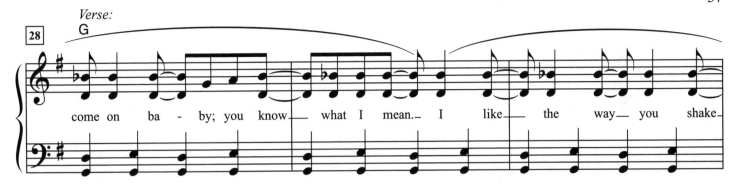

come on ba - by; you know___ what I mean.___ I like___ the way___ you shake___

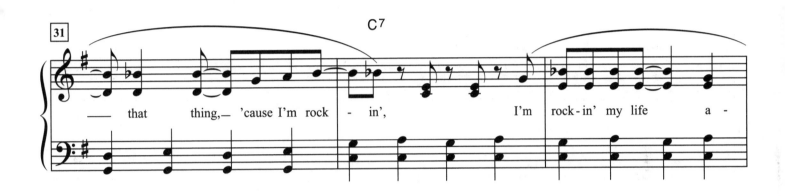

___ that thing,___ 'cause I'm rock - in', I'm rock-in' my life a -

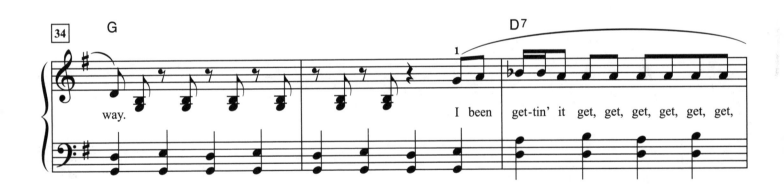

way. I been get-tin' it get, get, get, get, get, get,

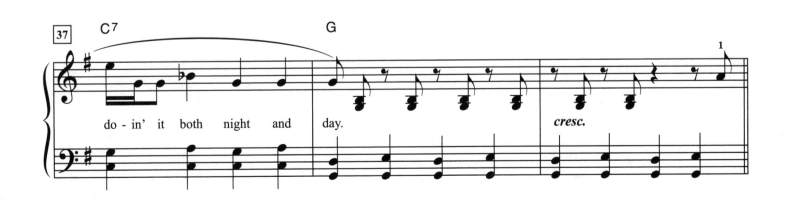

do - in' it both night and day.

cresc.

38

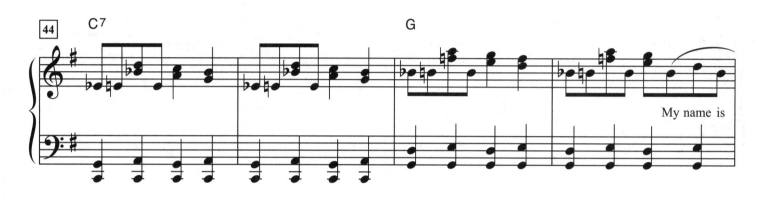

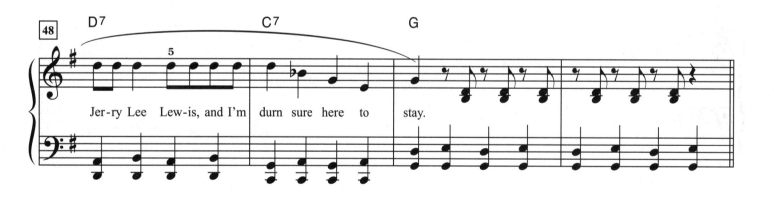

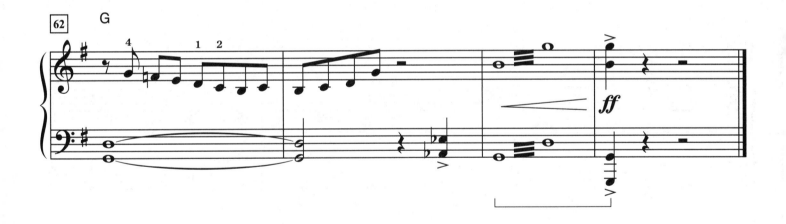
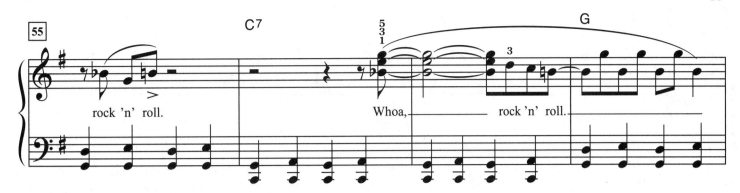
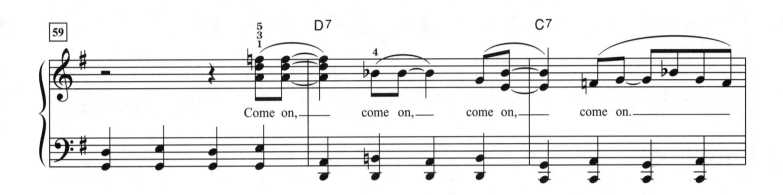

39

Verse 2:
I got a gal called Nelly; she's a chili pepper hot.
She knows how to roll; The Killer knows how to rock.
And I'm rock-in', rock-in' my life away.
I been rockin' and a-rollin' and a-movin' both night and day.

Verse 3:
Well, a streamline, fleetliner, military brass;
You know the general's daughter, but The Killer's top class.
I'm rockin', rockin' my life away.
I been movin' and groovin' and gettin' it both night and day.

OVER THE RAINBOW

Music by Harold Arlen
Lyric by E.Y. Harburg
Arranged by Bruce Nelson

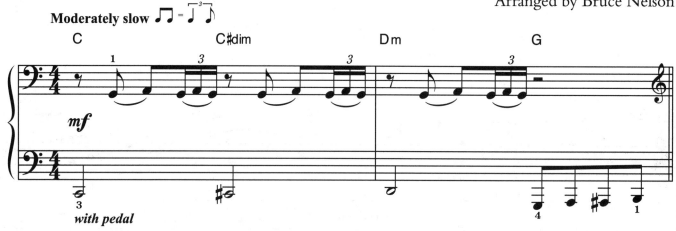

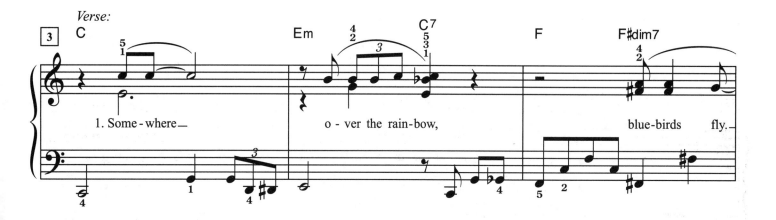

1. Some-where— o-ver the rain-bow, blue-birds fly.

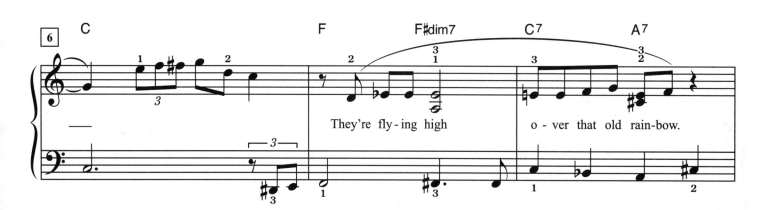

They're fly-ing high o-ver that old rain-bow.

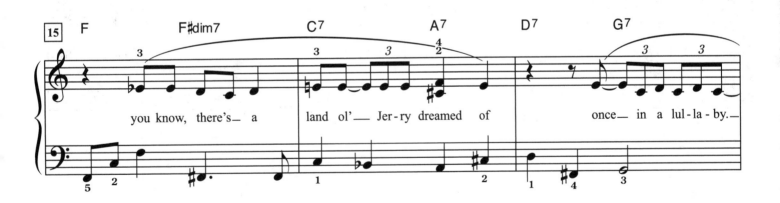

42

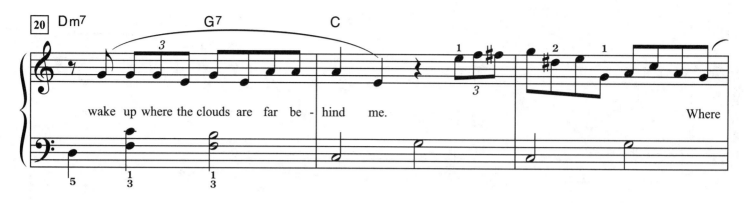

wake up where the clouds are far be - hind me.   Where

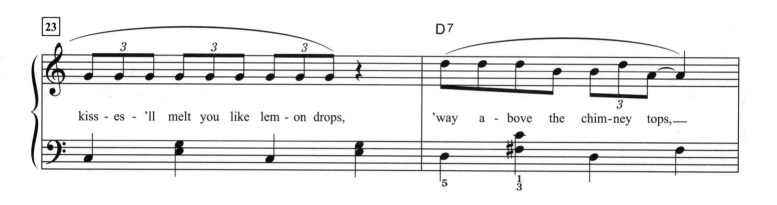

kiss - es - 'll melt you like lem - on drops,   'way a - bove the chim - ney tops,—

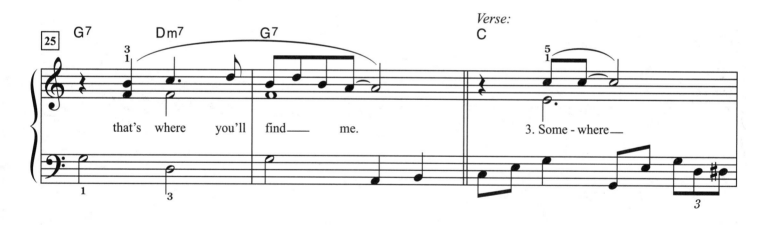

that's where you'll find—— me.   3. Some - where——

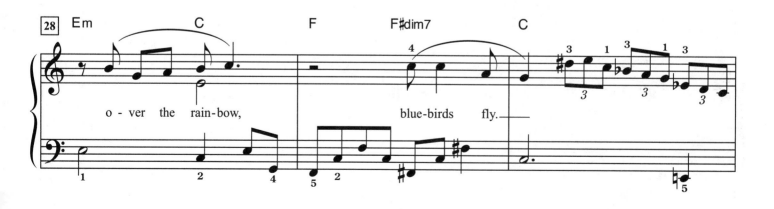

o - ver the rain-bow,   blue-birds   fly.—

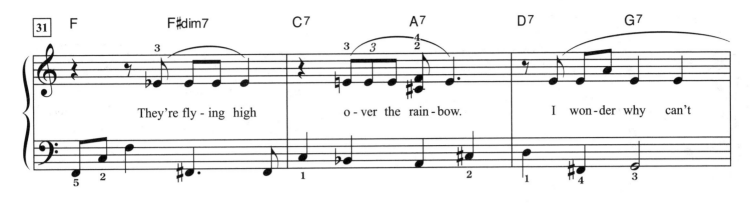

They're fly - ing high   o - ver the rain - bow.   I won - der why   can't

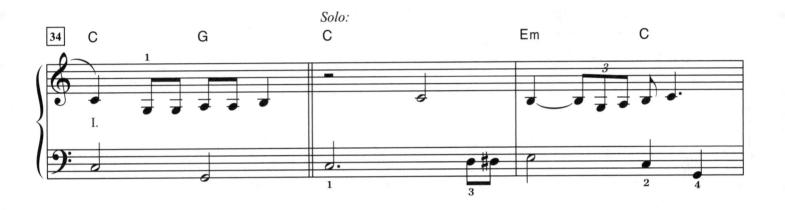

Solo:

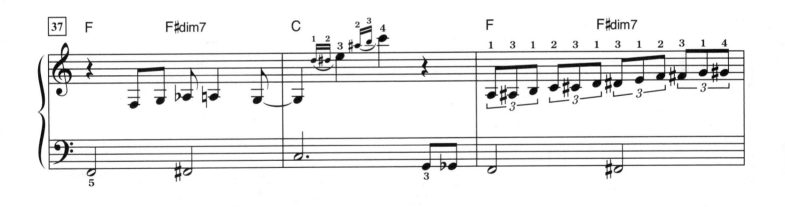

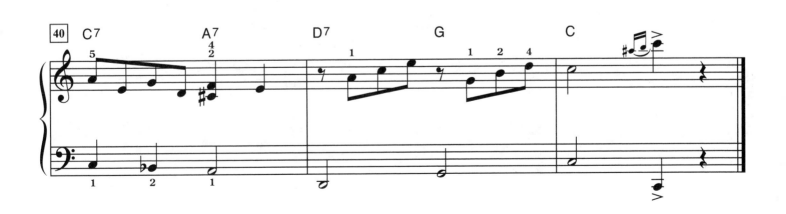

WHAT'D I SAY

Words and Music by Ray Charles
Arranged by Bruce Nelson

46

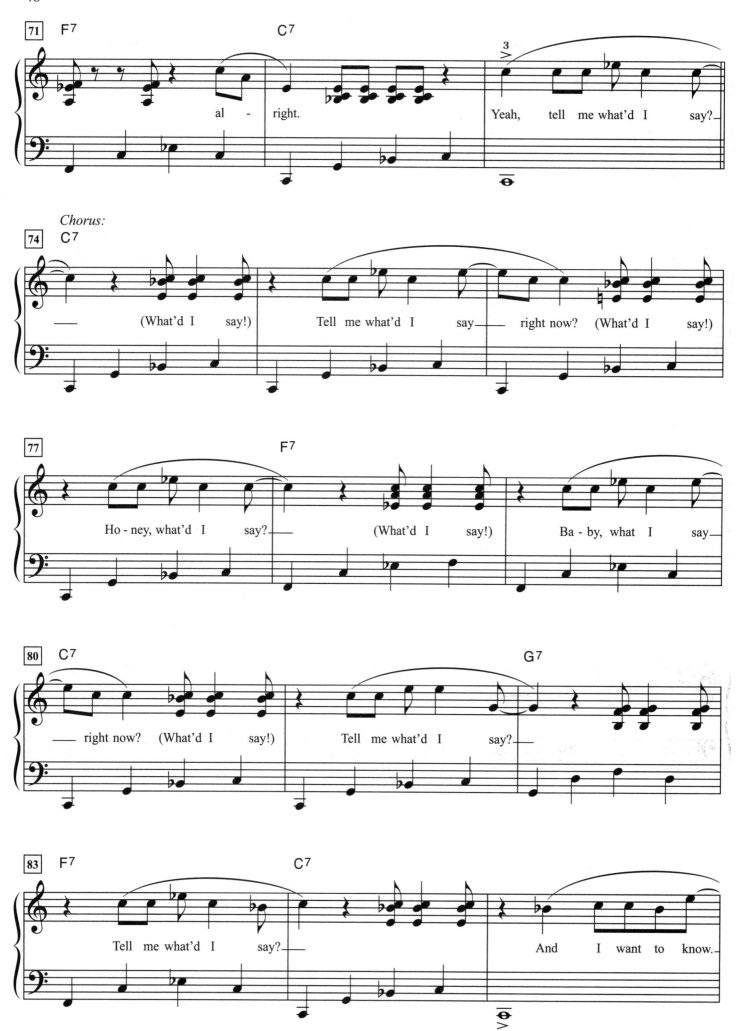

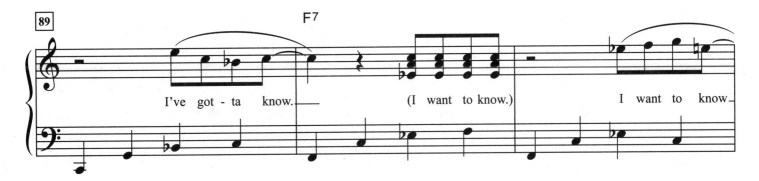

Verse 2:
See the gal with the diamond ring.
She knows how to shake that thing.
Alright, hey-hey,
Huh-huh, alright.

Verse 3:
Tell your mama, tell your pa,
I'm gonna send you back to Arkansas, haw, haw.
Hey, honey, you don't do right.
I say you don't do right.
Mmm, alright, yeah.
(To Solo:)

WHAT'S MADE MILWAUKEE FAMOUS
(HAS MADE A LOSER OUT OF ME)

Words and Music by Glenn Sutton
Arranged by Bruce Nelson

song. Then some-one buys an-oth-er round and, wher-

ev - er drinks— are free, what's made Mil-wau - kee

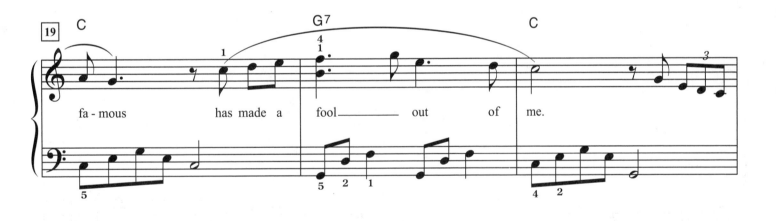

fa - mous has made a fool———— out of me.

Ba - by's begged me——— not to go———

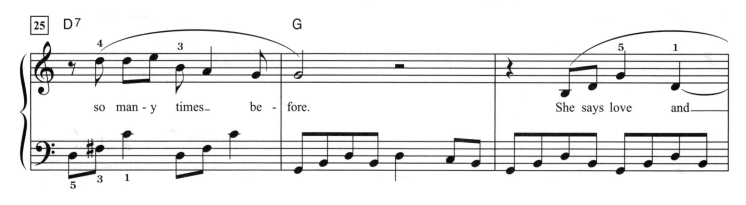

so man - y times be - fore.

She says love and

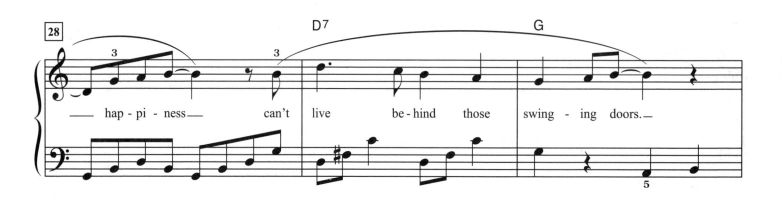

hap - pi - ness can't live be - hind those swing - ing doors.

Now she's gone and I'm to blame, too late, I fi - n'lly

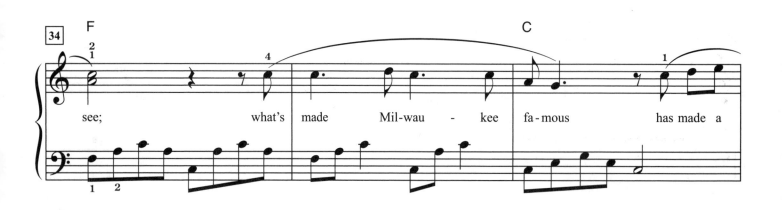

see; what's made Mil - wau - kee fa - mous has made a

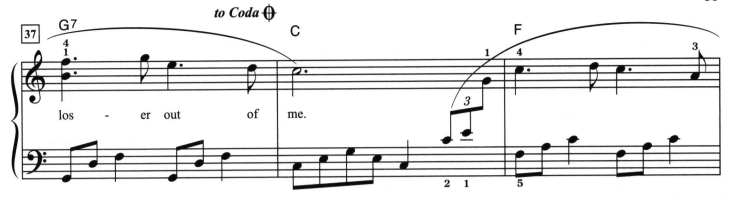

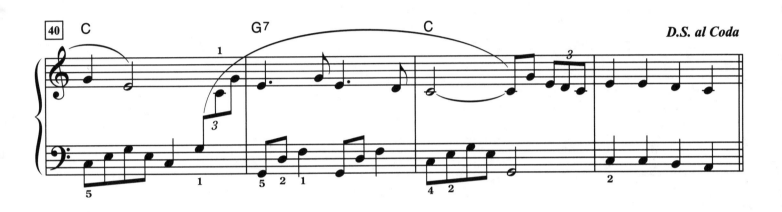

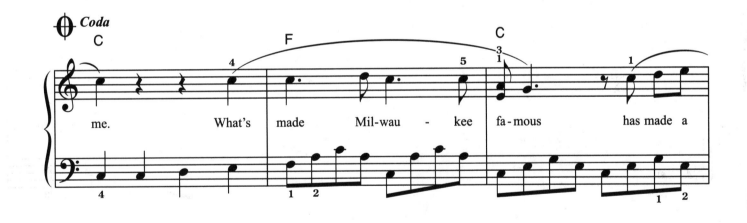

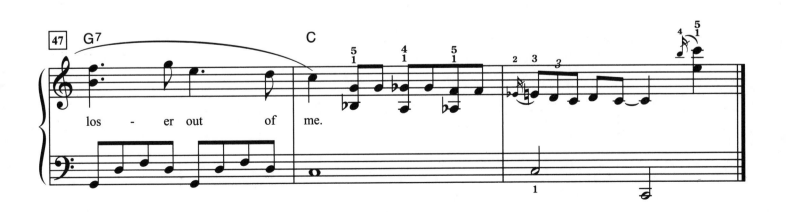

WHOLE LOTTA SHAKIN' GOING ON

Words and Music by David Williams
Arranged by Bruce Nelson

Moderately fast rock and roll

Verse:

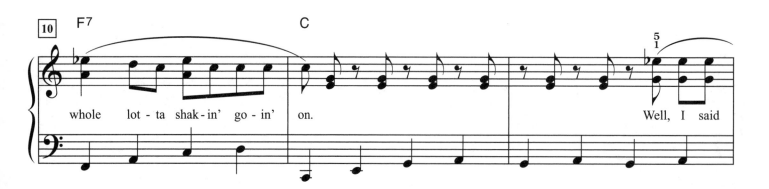

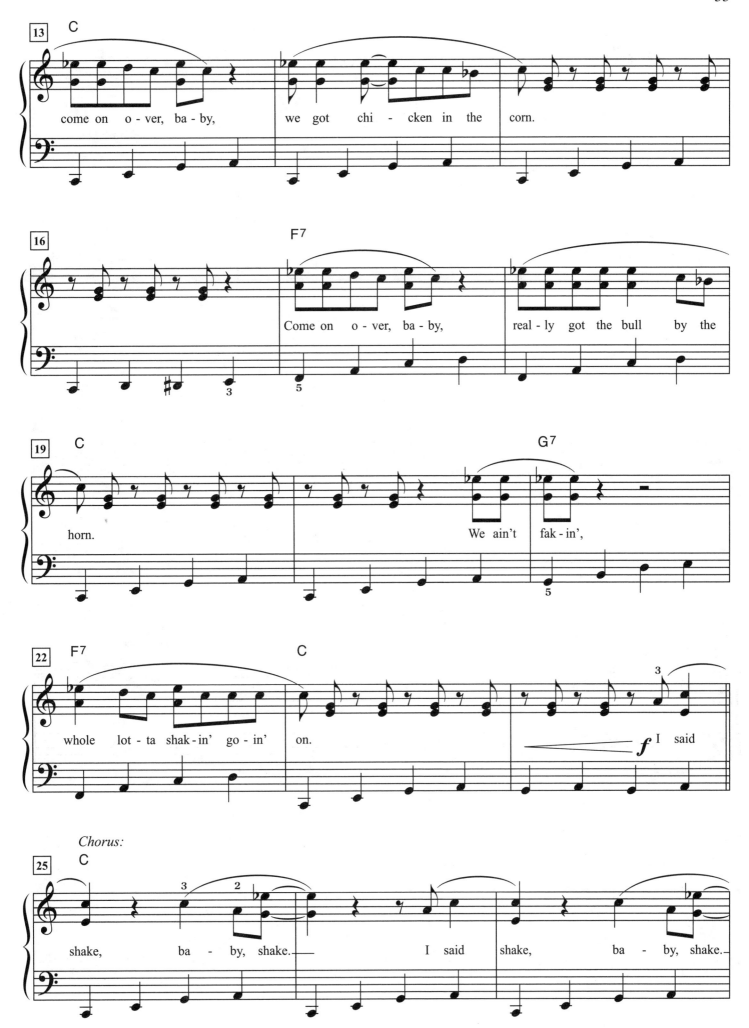

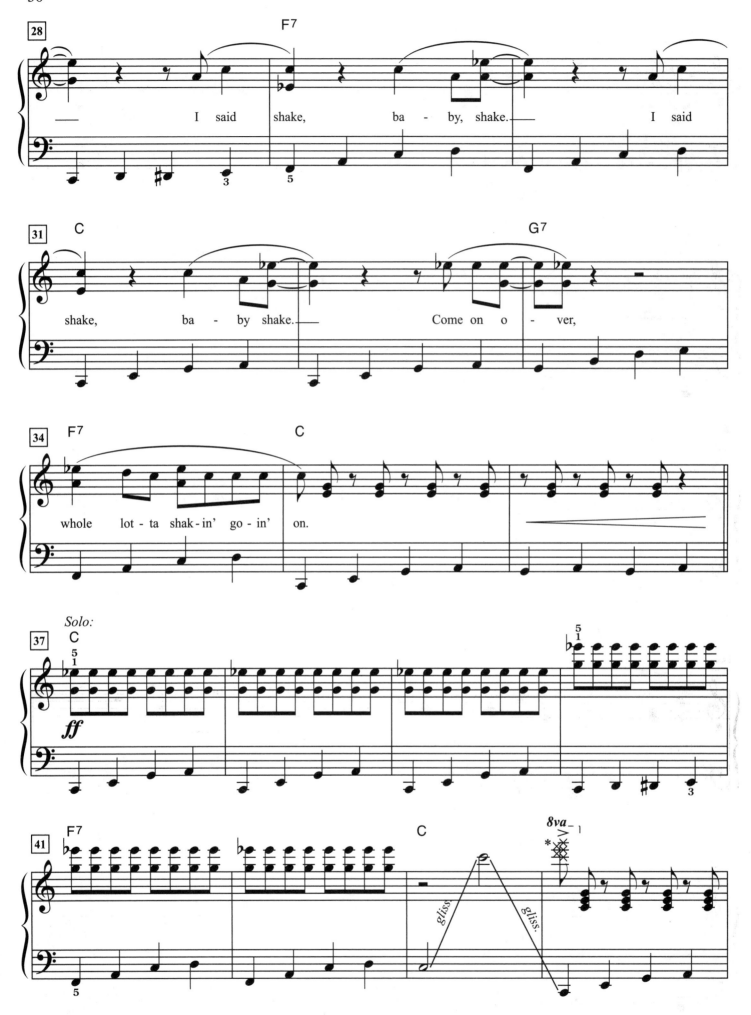

* In performance, Jerry Lee Lewis was known to have played this cluster with his foot.

58

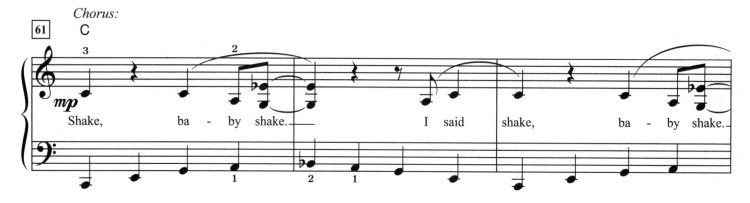

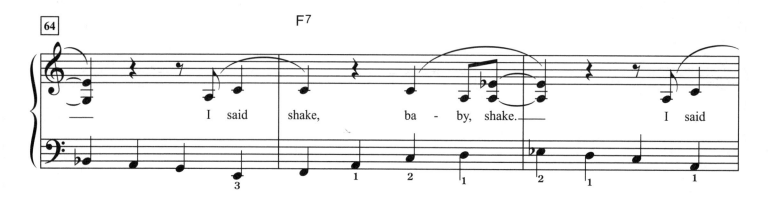

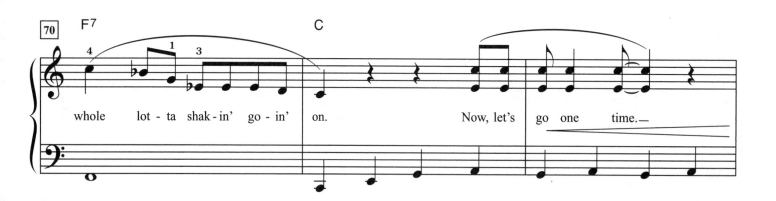

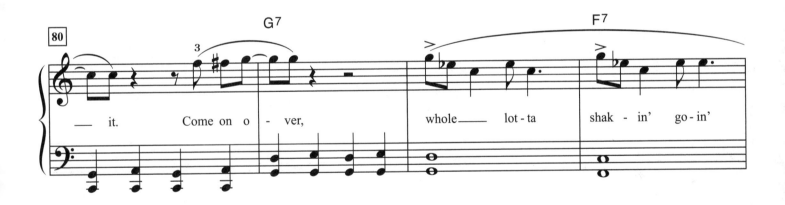

* In performance, Jerry Lee Lewis was known to have sat on the keys at this point.